Due Diligence: How to Research a Stock

Mariusz Skonieczny

Investment Publishing

Mariusz Skonieczny/Investment Publishing
1202 Far Pond Cir
Mishawaka, IN 46544
www.classicvalueinvestors.com

Ordering Information:
Quantity sales. Special discounts are available on quantity purchases by corporations, associations, and others. For details, contact the "Special Sales Department" at the address above.

Due Diligence: How to Research a Stock/ Mariusz Skonieczny.
—1st ed.
ISBN 978-0-9848490-3-1

Table of Contents

Preface

Preface

In 2012, I released my Value Investing University DVD Collection and received a positive response from investors all over the world. The collection included 10 DVDs, one of which was Due Diligence: Researching a Stock. Some of the feedback that I received was that investors wished that the Due Diligence video was also available in a book format because this is how they are used to consuming information.

So, after three years, I have decided to write a separate book on due diligence. This book contains some of the same information as the DVD, but it is expanded. Obviously, the book does not provide you with the same visual experience, but it gives you more detailed explanation.

Due diligence is something that can be intimidating for investors. It doesn't have to be like this. Due diligence is simply a process that you go through to learn about a business so that you can decide whether to purchase its stock. There is no one correct way of doing it just like there is no one correct way of inspecting a house.

Through this book, all I am doing is sharing with you a method of due diligence that makes sense to me and the one I developed over several years of studying companies. You can use it as a guide and stick to it 100 percent or you can take some parts and develop your own process. It is really up to you. However, if you are new to investing, it is helpful to have someone hold your hand until you feel comfortable doing it on your own. Treat this book as a set of training wheels to use until you can ride by yourself.

CHAPTER 1

Introduction

CHAPTER 1

Introduction

In this day and age, we are overloaded with all kinds of information, including financial information. The problem is not finding investment ideas but deciding which ones are worth studying. If you don't have some kind of process or screening method, then you will waste a lot of time researching companies that you should have eliminated during the first half hour.

I like to divide my due diligence into three parts—quick due diligence, medium due diligence, and full due diligence. Quick due diligence is a process that should only take you about 10 minutes. During this stage, you will gather just enough facts to quickly assess whether it is worth moving on to medium due diligence, which is more detailed and should take you about one hour. If you still like the stock after these first two steps, then you can move on to the final step which is full due diligence. In this step, you really study the company in detail. It usually takes me anywhere between three and seven days to complete the full due diligence process. Depending on how many hours per day you dedicate to investing, it might take you longer than that. After you complete all three stages, then you will be able to decide whether you want to purchase a particular stock.

CHAPTER 2

Quick Due Diligence

CHAPTER 2

Quick Due Diligence

After you learn about a stock, you should perform a brief analysis to see if you are even remotely interested in the company. You don't want to waste hours and hours on a particular company only to find that it operates in an industry that you want to avoid or that it has a level of debt that concerns you. By quickly eliminating companies that do not appeal to you, you can instead spend your time on companies that interest you.

The goal of quick due diligence is to answer the following questions:

- What kind of business is the company in?
- Is the company profitable?
- Does it have any debt?
- What did its stock chart look like over the last five years?
- Are the insiders buying stock?

- Have any shareholders filed Schedules 13D or 13G recently?
- Are there any recent press releases that stand out?
- Does its stock look cheap?

Let's take a look at how to answer these questions.

What kind of business is the company in?

To find out what kind of business the company operates in, type the ticker symbol into Google Finance and scroll down to read a short description. Then, under Website Links, visit the company's website and look it over quickly to see what it is that the company does.

You want to find out what type of business the company is involved in because it gives you an idea of what kind of stock you are dealing with. You might not understand the business yet but this is not important. What is important is that the learning process starts with gaining incremental knowledge with each step you take.

Is the company profitable?

To quickly determine whether the company is profitable, I like to go directly to EDGAR (the US Securities and Exchange Commission's Electronic Data Gathering, Analysis, and Retrieval system) and find its most recent filing of Form 10-K, which is the company's annual report as submitted to the SEC. I then go directly to the income statement. You can also take a quick look at the financials on Morningstar.com by entering its ticker symbol.

You are finding out whether the company is profitable not because you should only invest in profitable companies but because it will give you an idea of what the company's situation is. Unprofitable companies can only stay unprofitable for so long. Something has to happen for them to survive—they either have to become profitable, liquidate, sell to a different company, or raise more money. At this point, you don't need to know these things. All you need to know is whether the company makes money or not.

Does it have any debt?

To find out whether the company has any debt, all you have to do is skim through the balance sheet under the liabilities section. I personally do not like to invest in companies that have a lot of debt so I am able to quickly eliminate them in this step. There is no rule on how much debt is too much but I like zero debt or very little in relation to equity.

You don't have to have the same rules as I do about debt. Yes, investing in companies with debt increases the risk, but at the right time debt can be beneficial. For example, if you are good at timing the market, then you can buy companies with lots of debt right before they turn and make a boatload of money because debt provides you with financial leverage. I, however, am terrible at timing the market so I stick with companies that do not have a lot of debt.

What did its stock chart look like over the last five years?

I like looking at the chart just to see how the stock has been trading. I am not doing it to perform any technical analysis because I don't believe in it, but a chart paints a certain picture. For example, if I look at a chart showing a significant price drop in a short period of time, I know that something bad must have happened to cause it. Was it a negative earnings report or something else? I don't know and I don't care right now, but I want to keep it in mind so I can look into it.

If I see that the stock price is down 90 percent over the last five years, I know that investors have gone through a lot of pain. They could be so exhausted from losing money that they no longer care whether there is any value left or whether the company is turning around. They just want out at any price.

Are the insiders buying stock?

To check whether insiders are buying the company's stock, use the SEC's EDGAR website to see whether Form 4 has been filed. Insiders must file Form 4 after they purchase their company's stock. Through this filing you can see the individuals that are buying, how many shares they are buying, the price paid, the dollar value of the transaction, and how many shares they own following the transaction.

To make this step even faster, you can use InsiderCow.com instead of EDGAR. InsiderCow is a free website that allows you to enter a company's ticker symbol to see insider transactions. The website displays the transactions in an easy-to-read format while EDGAR makes you work hard to see the same information.

One thing that I would like to point out is this—I like to see insiders buy because it tells me that they think the stock is cheap. However, if I see insiders sell, it does not mean that the stock is overvalued. Peter Lynch once said, "Insiders might sell their shares for any number of reasons, but they buy them for only one: they think the price will rise."

Insiders might sell because they are buying a house or funding a child's college education. So, just because they are selling doesn't necessarily mean you should rule the company out. However, if they are selling, it is definitely good to know about it.

Have any shareholders filed Schedules 13D or 13G recently?

Anyone that acquires more than five percent of any class of a company's shares is required to file either Schedule 13D or 13G with the SEC within 10 days of the transaction. Schedule 13D is a longer form than 13G. In order to be able to file Schedule 13G, the filer has to demonstrate that the investment is only passive. Schedule 13D is used by activist investors who are looking to push for changes.

To find out whether there have been any filings of Schedules 13D or 13G, go to EDGAR and search for company filings though the company's name or ticker symbol. You will see lots of different filings, so skim through them until you see either Schedule 13D or 13G. If you see these filings, then it means that there are significant buyers who are accumulating the company's stock. If they are buying, there must be a reason for it. They probably think that the stock is undervalued. This is good news for you because you are also interested in buying undervalued stocks.

Are there any recent press releases that stand out?

Companies are like living organisms meaning that something is always happening. When that something is meaningful, it must be disclosed to investors in the form of press releases or filings of Form 8-K.

I usually like to skim through press releases on the company's website under the investor relations section. However, you can also get them from other sources. Enter the ticker symbol at Yahoo Finance or Google Finance and you will also be able to see the latest press releases on these sites. This can save you time if you know the ticker symbol but don't have the website address handy.

I look through the headlines of press releases because I can quickly find out certain information. Is the company being investigated, sued, or delisted? Did it release a new product or sign a major client? Skimming through press releases quickly gives you an idea of what is happening without investing a lot of time.

Does its stock look cheap?

To find out whether the stock might be a bargain, look at its chart. If the stock price has collapsed over the last few years, it will appear to be cheap in relation to the past. However, if the stock price has gone up over the past few years, it does not necessarily mean that it is not cheap. There might be more room left for appreciation.

You can also look at the P/E ratio. Is it low or ridiculously high? Obviously, low P/E ratios of approximately 10 to 13 are preferable. However, a company's P/E ratio alone does not tell you much, although it is good to know. Go back to the company's income statement and look at how much the company makes in operating income or net income and compare it to the market cap. What is the market cap to operating income or net income multiple? Look at the operating income and net income from previous years and compare them to the current market cap. Repeat the same calculation with these figures.

For example, if the current net income is $1 million while the market cap is $100 million, then the market cap to net income multiple is 100. This appears to be expensive. However, if a prior year's net income was $50 million and you compare it to the current market cap of $100 million, you get a multiple of two, which means that if the company can return to making that level of net income, the stock could be incredibly cheap.

Look at the shareholders' equity and compare it to the market cap. Ideally, the shareholder's equity should be higher than the market cap. However, in certain industries it is not possible. Some industries are asset light and comparing the shareholders' equity with the market cap will not yield any meaningful conclusions. However, for insurance stocks, the comparison between the two variables is important.

Look at how much cash the company has and compare it to the market cap. How much of the company's market cap is in cash? If the company is profitable, then a large cash hoard is not that important but if it is losing money, then cash helps the company survive bad times.

Right now, you are not really trying to value the company. You are just trying to get an idea of whether there is a possibility of undervaluation.

CHAPTER 3

Medium Due Diligence

CHAPTER 3

Medium Due Diligence

Quick due diligence is intended to allow you to quickly look at a company and decide whether you are kind of interested. Medium due diligence is just a step further. It takes you deeper into your research but it still does not take you to a full-blown analysis. This step should take you about an hour and afterward, you will have a very good idea of whether you want to study the company in detail.

Insider Buying

In the previous step, you learned whether insiders are buying. If they are, pay attention to who they are. It is very good if the CEO and CFO are buying. Check how much they recently bought in relation to what they already own. This information is all included on InsiderCow.

Also, how do their purchases compare to how much they make in compensation for running the company? To find out the compensation, go to EDGAR, open the most recent proxy filings, and scroll all the way to the compensation table. If the recent buy represents a good chunk of what the insider makes per year, then this is good news for you because it increases the probability of the stock being undervalued.

If the insider purchases are done by directors, do a quick search to learn who the directors are. It can be very helpful. For example, Mitcham Industries is a company whose stock declined considerably after the price of oil collapsed. The company is involved in leasing oil and gas exploration equipment. Peter H. Blum is a director who buys the stock when it is trading really cheaply. When I looked at his past history (all on InsiderCow), I noticed that he is incredible at timing when to buy Mitcham's stock. A search for his name reveals that he is a former investment banker with 25 years of experience in the energy industry. This tells me that he knows what he is doing when it comes to buying and selling stocks. If he is buying Mitcham Industries, then I had better pay attention.

Schedules 13D or 13G

In the previous step, you also learned whether there are any other large investors, such as hedge funds, buying the stock when you checked for any filings of Schedules 13D or 13G. In medium due diligence, you want to find out who they are. Take their names and Google them. Many times, you will find that these buyers are companies with websites that talk about their investment philosophies. If they are value investors, then this is a good sign. See if you can find any interviews with them to learn more about them.

Some of them are very secretive and don't have websites, or if they are hedge funds, their websites are password protected. In this case, you won't be able to find out a lot but you should still try. Remember that hedge funds are in the business of attracting capital so they have to market themselves somehow. Many do so by granting interviews. YouTube is a great place to see if there are any recorded interviews. Also, these days, everybody has a Facebook and Twitter account. See what you can find out there. By looking through the person's tweets, you can figure out what kind of investor they are.

Also, on EDGAR, you can find out what else they are buying. This in itself is a great source of other investment ideas. If a particular hedge fund has more than $100 million of assets under management, it is required to file Form 13F quarterly. By accessing filings of this form, you can find out how many positions it has in its portfolio. The best case scenario is when the hedge fund owns just a few names and your company is on the list. This means it is likely that its managers have high conviction in your company as an investment opportunity. If, on the other hand, you learn that the hedge fund owns 100 stocks, then your subject company is just one of many. I usually ignore hedge funds that own so many positions.

Investment-Sharing Websites

If you have read my other books, then you should know that you can find investment ideas on investment-sharing websites such as Value Investors Club, SumZero, Distressed Debt Investors Club, and MicroCapClub. These websites should also be used for research purposes. When you have a particular company you are researching, try to see if anyone who writes for these websites has already written about it.

Another site that I did not talk about yet is Seeking Alpha. The website is a research platform with insight and analysis provided by investors instead of sell-side analysts. It was founded in 2004 by David Jackson, a former sell-side analyst with

Morgan Stanley. Some content is free and some is available only through a paid subscription. It didn't use to be like this. There was a time when all the content was free and Seeking Alpha was making money by advertising.

Seeking Alpha is great tool for finding investment articles on particular companies. You will often find that many different authors have written articles about the same company. I like it a lot when someone writes a bullish case and someone else writes a bearish case. This way, I find out the good and the bad about a company.

You want to read investment write-ups by other people because it is a free way to access other people's research. This saves you a lot of time.

I want to make one thing clear—reading reports by others is not a substitute for your own research because you have no idea how much research the author did and whether any errors were made. You want to use other people's research to gain an understanding of the companies you are studying. But you have to be aware that writers have many different reasons for why they are writing about various companies. Some write because they want to receive feedback from others. Others write because they want to market themselves or their businesses and they might not even own the stock themselves. For example, when someone writes an article about a company on Seeking Alpha, it shows up under the company's news in Google Finance and Yahoo Finance. This means that many people end up reading it and it provides great exposure for the author. It is like a free advertisement for the author's book, newsletter, or whatever he is selling. Consequently, if the article was done solely for marketing purposes, do you want to trust it 100 percent and not do your own work? Probably not, but you can still learn from it.

Write-ups on the Value Investors Club, SumZero, or MicroCapClub websites are most likely done by an author who owns the stock or whose employer owns the stock. This is better than if the author did not own it (on Seeking Alpha, the author discloses his ownership status). However, these websites are not without problems. Authors on these sites are required to write a certain number of investment ideas per year to maintain their membership. Most of them would not write anything if they were not forced to because they are investors, not writers. Because of this dynamic, they might submit a poorly written report.

The bottom line is this—read their work to learn from it but do not consider it to be sufficient research.

Company's Website

In the previous step, you briefly visited the company's website, but now it's time to go back and take a second look. This time, spend more time on it. Look around. Try to see if you can find information about the company's history, products and services, and the management's biographical descriptions. Also, some companies now have YouTube channels. Watch some of their videos. All of this helps you to become more familiar with the company's business, and each item you look at gives you a little bit more knowledge.

Finally, look for a section called Investor Relations. This is where you will find annual reports, conference calls, press releases, and various presentations.

Annual Report

Once you have looked at the Investor Relations part of the website, find the most recent annual report and read it from cover to cover. Some of these reports will start with a letter to shareholders summarizing the year, its successes and failures. Then, read the rest of the report. Pay attention to the company's description, its products and services, competitiveness, financial data, and risk factors. The first time I look at an annual report, I usually read the headings under the "Risk Factors" section and I look for certain types of risks. For example, I don't like to invest in companies that have the majority of their revenues coming from just a few customers because if they lose one of them, it will be devastating. Consequently, I will usually eliminate a company once I find out that, let's say, 70 percent of its revenue comes from two customers. However, if the company is growing fast and is in the process of diversifying its client base, then its large customer concentration might be only transitory.

You will find some annual reports easier to understand than others. This is normal. The more you know about particular businesses, the easier it is to read and understand their reports. You do not have to comprehend everything the first time you read a particular report.

If you cannot find annual reports on the company's website, you can also access them through EDGAR. In this case, you will look for Form 10-K filings, which are required to be filed with the SEC by publicly traded companies.

Investor Presentation

Sometimes in the Investor Relations section of the company's website you will find an investor presentation that was put together by the management. In this presentation, they make their case for why you should invest in their company. In other words, it is the company's advertisement intended to sell you on the idea of investing in their stock. This is useful information because it shows you the main reasons why the management thinks that investing in their company's stock is a good idea.

Many times, the management uses the same presentation when they attend various investment conferences. It is not usual to find an investor presentation accompanied by a video recording from an investment conference. Reading the presentation and watching any related video are extremely useful and important parts of your due diligence.

CHAPTER 4

Full Due Diligence

CHAPTER 4

Full Due Diligence

After spending a couple of hours performing both quick and medium due diligence, you should have a pretty good idea of whether a particular company is worthy of a place in your investment portfolio. Depending on the market, you might have to perform quick and medium due diligence on several companies before you find one that is enticing enough to progress toward full due diligence. During bear markets when stocks are cheap, you might have to look at only two or three companies before you decide to study them fully while during bull markets when stocks are expensive, you might have to look at ten or more before you find the right candidate for full due diligence. Once you find one, then it really is time to go to work.

Unlike the other two steps, performing full due diligence is much more intense and time consuming. I would say that if you work on it every day for several hours, it should take you about a week. If you are unwilling to put this much work into studying companies, then you should think twice about whether you should be managing your money.

I want you to think of full due diligence in this way. If you were to open a business, whether it be a restaurant, hair salon, or some kind of manufacturing company, and you did not have any experience in that business, what would be the first thing that you would do?

If you are smart, you would probably start learning about the business that you want to enter, which would require reading books, trade magazines, news articles, and also talking to people in the industry. This seems obvious, right? Well, it is not so obvious to stock market investors because most of them have absolutely no idea about what they own in their portfolios.

Whether you start a business or buy into an existing business through the purchase of a company's stock, you have to go through the same process, which means you have to learn about the industry and the specific business.

Learning about the Industry

By now, you should know what the company does and what industry it is in. If you are having trouble locating the industry, look it up on EDGAR. Every public company in the US has a specific industry number assigned to it through the Standard Industrial Classification code system (SIC). If you have already studied the industry before, you can obviously skip this part, but if you have not, this is when you need to learn about it.

I usually like to start with Amazon to search for various books on the industry. For example, when I first looked at International Speedway Corporation, which is a promoter of NASCAR races, I didn't know anything about the business of auto racing. I knew that people go to races to watch cars drive around in circles but that was about it. Before I invested in the company, I had to learn about NASCAR as a business.

I went to Amazon to see what kinds of books were available on this topic. When I typed in "Business NASCAR," I found several books:

- *The 200-MPH Billboard: The Insider Story of How Big Money Changed NASCAR*, by Mark Yost
- *One Helluva Ride: How NASCAR Swept the Nation*, by Liz Clarke

- *The NASCAR Way: The Business That Drives the Sport*, by Robert G. Hagstrom
- *Growing Up NASCAR: Racing's Most Outrageous Promoter Tells All*, by Humpy Wheeler and Peter Golenbock

I read all of these books and because of them, I gained a deep understanding of the industry and the companies operating within this industry. I understood why the sport became so popular, why TV stations and advertisers paid so much money to be associated with the NASCAR brand, why it was pretty much impossible for a new player to start promoting NASCAR races, and much more.

Because of these books, I was able to read and understand the annual reports of all the companies in the industry without any problem. I understood how they made money and why the margins were what they were.

I find it almost impossible to understand companies' annual reports unless I am familiar with the industry. Yes, there are exceptions. When companies are very simple, then reading the annual report is easy, but even then, attempts to comply with complicated regulation can result in language that is difficult to understand.

Let me give you another example. Let's say you are interested in Bridgepoint Education, which is a for-profit post-secondary educational institution. It is a competitor of the University of Phoenix. If you don't know anything about the for-profit education industry, go to Amazon and type in "for-profit education" to see what is available.

If you perform that search, you will find:

- *Higher Ed, Inc.: The Rise of the For-Profit University*, by Richard S. Ruch
- *For-Profit Colleges and Universities*, by Guilbert C. Hentschke, et. al
- *University, Inc.: The Corporate Corruption of Higher Education*, by Jennifer Washburn

As you can see, there are plenty of sources that we can use to learn about the for-profit education industry. But you might be thinking, "I can't buy several books every time I want to study a company." Don't worry, many times you won't have to buy them. You can search for these books on Amazon and check if your local library has them or whether the library can borrow them from a different library.

If you can't find any books on a particular industry, you can obviously use the Internet. If you are investing in a restaurant stock, search on Google for various topics such as "starting a restaurant," "restaurant industry," or "how to be a successful restaurateur." You can learn a great deal by doing this.

I also like to use YouTube to learn about industries. For example, one company I studied in the past was Heckmann Corporation, which is a water solutions business for the fracking industry. At the time, I had absolutely no idea what was meant by water solutions and I definitely did not know what fracking was. Within four hours of watching videos on YouTube, I was an expert on fracking and why the company's services were so important to its clients. Then, when I was reading the company's annual report, I knew exactly what they were talking about. The same thing applies to viewing investor presentations. I was able to follow point by point and understand what everything meant. Without watching those YouTube videos, I would have been completely lost and probably would have moved on to a different company.

How about Netflix? You can find many movies on companies and industries. Netflix has lots of useful content such as documentaries or biographies. If you want to learn about the food industry, Netflix has:

- *Inside Chipotle*
- *Food, Inc.*
- *Super Size Me*
- *Fat, Sick & Nearly Dead*
- *Hungry for Change*

There is so much available. I am surprised at how little investors are aware of what is on Netflix. They have no problem bidding up Netflix's stock price to the stratosphere but they won't look into its service to help them learn about businesses and industries. I love watching documentaries.

CEO Interviews on the Internet

Search the Internet and YouTube for any interviews with the CEO of the company you are researching. You can search for "Company ABC CEO Interview," or "Company ABC Name of CEO Interview." I like interviews because you usually learn things that you would never learn from any other sources. If the CEO is the founder, he can tell you how the company was started, what kind of struggles it faced, where it is going, and much more. I also search for interviews with former CEOs. This gives you an idea of how the company evolved. Maybe it had a different strategy in the past and learning about it enables you to put the pieces of the puzzle together. For example, your company may have sold a particular business division, and because you heard the former CEO discuss it in an interview, you can understand why they chose to sell when you read about it in an annual report.

It is so much easier to understand the business and the management after you read, watch, or listen to some of their interviews. Also, you get to know their personalities.

Search Google

I also like to just type the name of the company into Google's search box and see what kind of results are returned. I will usually look through the first 500 results. I don't read them all but I do read the ones that catch my eye and help me learn about the company. You'd be surprised how many things you can learn about a company by performing this type of research. You can learn about current and past lawsuits, customer complaints, analyst reports, and much, much more.

Also, perform an advanced search on Google for PDF documents. You will be surprised how many reports you will find on the company that did not come up under the previous search results. You might find a detailed analysis on the company done by hedge fund managers, newsletter writers, or even students from various universities. Recently, I was researching Breeze-Eastern Corporation and I searched Google for PDF documents about the company and I found a detailed analysis done by an investment club at a university.

FundingUniverse.com

I believe that learning about a company's history is extremely important. FundingUniverse.com is a website that provides a short list of basic facts, such as when the company was founded and how many employees it has, as well as written descriptions about its history. It is amazing how much you can find on this website.

By reading about a company's history, you learn about why things are the way they are. You might learn how the company's flagship product evolved from another product that has become obsolete. Or, you might learn about the origins of the company's culture. If you are puzzled by why the company is located in a particular city or state, you might learn that this is because the founder was born there or his biggest client lived there.

Read Message Boards

Now that so much information is available on the Internet, people share opinions about various publicly traded companies on message boards such as InvestorsHub and Yahoo Message Boards. You should spend about an hour or so reading what other investors have to say about the company. Often, you will find completely useless comments, but there will also be ones that you can learn from.

You will find people who have been following the company for quite some time, and they might have something useful to say, such as a short analysis explaining why the company is cheap, or why the management is incompetent.

As with anything else in life, when people are satisfied with something, they will probably not say anything but when they are dissatisfied with something, they will let you know. This happens with stocks—when some investors become aggravated for whatever reason, they might go to one of these message boards to voice their complaints, and this kind of feedback is extremely useful if you are thinking about investing in the company that they are talking about.

Also, if you have a question, you can post your own comment and you may receive an intelligent response. You have nothing to lose. One time, I was researching a company and I saw that the CEO was buying shares but I didn't know why. To quickly find out whether the company was worth pursuing, I submitted a comment on one of these boards asking other investors if they could tell me in a few paragraphs why they liked the company. I received more than one response and it saved me a lot of time.

Glassdoor.com

Imagine if you were interested in a particular company and you had a friend working there. You would probably ask this person about the company and what it is like to work there. Well, you can get almost the same type of feedback by going to Glassdoor.com where employees write reviews about how they like or dislike working for a particular company. This is one of the best ways to find out about the culture within the company and how employees are being treated. If the company does not treat its employees with respect, you might want to think twice about investing in it because the management may also mistreat you as a shareholder.

Employees who write reviews on Glassdoor.com do not have to reveal their names. This way, they can express their opinions without the fear of getting fired. With that being said, because of the anonymity, they can also exaggerate their negative comments. This is why you want to read many reviews and do other research to get a more balanced picture.

EDGAR

As you already know, EDGAR is a website run by the Securities and Exchange Commission. When publicly traded companies submit documents to the SEC, EDGAR is a place where they can be accessed. While the website can seem a bit daunting to navigate, it shouldn't be. When you spend some time on it, you will get the hang of it.

If you need any help, I have a separate video on how to navigate EDGAR and it is part of the Value Investing University DVD collection. It is available on my website (ClassicValueInvestors.com) or on Amazon.

Anyway, once you are on EDGAR, you want to access the three most important filings: Form 10-K, Form 10-Q, and DEF 14A.

Form 10-K

The first document that I want to read is the 10-K. In the previous step, you already read it once, but now you have a lot more knowledge about the company and industry, and it will be much easier to read it again. After reading it the second time, you want to be able to answer the following questions:

What products and services does the company provide and how do they satisfy their clients?

The key to being a successful investor is to really understand the company's products and services. We all buy things because we want to satisfy our needs or desires. We don't just give money away for nothing. We want things in return. The same principle applies to businesses—clients buy products and services because they have a need or a want. You need to put yourself in the shoes of the clients and figure out how the products and services satisfy them. You also have to think ahead and consider whether these products will continue to satisfy them in five to 10 years or whether they will need to be improved or replaced.

What countries does the company operate in?

Some companies do business domestically while others are international. Obviously, international companies have greater geographic diversification which can be viewed as less risky but at the same time, it can complicate the situation. International companies have to deal with different currencies, regulatory environments, cultures, and local competitors.

Domestic companies, on the other hand, might have a simplified business model, but as a result of focusing only on one country, they might have limited growth opportunities.

When was it founded?

It is a known fact that most new businesses fail, but the ones that succeed can make their investors wealthy. If your company was founded many years ago and is still around, then it has a track record of providing products or services that are wanted by its clients. If you are a conservative investor, then you should focus on such companies because they are more likely to limit losses. At the same time, you cannot expect huge home runs because a lot of the success is already priced in. However, if you are a more adventurous investor, then investing in newer companies might be right for you. One thing is for sure—you always need to know how long your company has been around no matter what type of investor you are.

What kind of clients does the company have?

If you understand the company's products and services, then you should know what kind of clients the company has. Also, you should know which portion of the market the company targets. For example, if you are a real estate agent, what kind of agent are you? Do you cater to the rich and famous or do you sell to the average guy? You can't treat the two different types of clientele the same way. It is no different for businesses. If you don't know the type of clients that the company has, how can you know whether the products or services are satisfying them?

How does the company market its products?

Many investors overlook this topic because they never had to make a business successful. I have seen many businesses that have failed simply because the cost of acquiring clients was so great. The point is, don't just skip over this section. Know how effective the company is at marketing.

Who are the customers?

Sometimes the 10-K filings list individual customers. Other times, these customers are listed in investor presentations. Are these customers leaders in their field or are they the weakest players? There are no hard rules about this. There are companies who specialize in servicing the top players and there are others who cater to the rest. What is important is that if your company pursues a strategy of targeting the top players, then it had better have top-tier clients, otherwise there is a disconnect.

Does the company make its products or does it outsource production?

Some companies manufacture their own products and others let someone else do the manufacturing. If the manufacturing is done in house, then the whole production process can be controlled more easily. However, at other times, it makes more sense to outsource manufacturing if the company does not have the capability to do it in house. There is no way of knowing which one is better without studying the industry and seeing what other players are doing.

What is its business strategy?

Publicly traded companies have to be run differently than private companies. With private companies, owners can simply run them for cash flow to support their lifestyles. With public companies, this would not go over too well. Wall Street is obsessed with growth. Consequently, your company must have some kind of business strategy or plan for how they are going to make you money. Then, you can decide on your own if you believe in the strategy or not by buying the stock or staying away.

Does the company have a competitive advantage? Is so, what is it?

Companies that have advantages over competitors have what Warren Buffett has described as a moat. The competitive advantage, whether it be a great brand, sheer size, or switching costs, should translate into high margins and/or a high return on equity. When I say "high," I mean in relation to its competitors.

When you study one company, you should also learn about some of its competitors. If they are also public, then their filings will also be available on EDGAR, assuming they are US companies.

Does the company operate in a very competitive industry?

This is easy to find out. Companies will clearly state this in their 10-K filings. If the industry is extremely competitive, you know that the players fight with each other to win and maintain clients. You had better make sure your company stays competitive.

Is the industry fragmented or does it have a few leaders?

There are certain industries that are fragmented. The logistics industry is a prime example of this. Competitors within the logistics industry service clients in particular regions, and there are not very many visible leaders nationwide. It is not unusual to see companies acquiring each other in order to grow and gain access to client lists.

Where does the company get its raw materials from for the production of its products?

Suppliers are an important element in making businesses successful. If you don't have tomatoes, you can't make pizza. Pay attention to the types of companies or industries that supply materials to your company. Are supply disruptions likely to occur? Can suppliers easily raise prices? Does the company have many suppliers to choose from or is there only one supplier that must be relied upon?

Does the company have multiple business segments in more than one industry?

Just because you associate one type of business with a company's name does not mean that it does not have any other business segments. Sometimes, they may be in completely different industries. As mentioned before, public companies have to keep growing or Wall Street will not be happy. Consequently, companies create or acquire new business segments. When this has been done many times, investors can become confused and have a difficult time understanding the parent entity. This can be an opportunity for you if you can understand the separate business segments. It is not unusual for one business segment to be worth more than the price of the entire parent company. Wall Street may not be paying attention because the other business segments may be obscuring its value. At some point, someone might force the management to sell the weak businesses in order to unlock value.

Is the product or service essential to its customers? Can they live without it?

Not all revenues are created equal. Some revenues are extremely reliable when the customers desperately need the product. Other revenues can disappear very quickly. For example, if parents encounter difficult times, they will cut their children's piano lessons in order to be able to put food on the table. Companies must make the same kinds of decisions when facing hard times.

How many employees does the company have?

When you study different companies you will notice that some business models rely heavily on labor while others are able to generate millions of dollars worth of revenue with just a handful of employees. When you look at the number of employees, pay attention to the workforce composition between part-time and full-time employees. Also, note how much revenue is generated per employee and how that compares to its competitors.

Do any customers represent a significant portion of the company's revenues?

Any business, whether it is public or private, wants big clients. Scoring a major client is something to celebrate. However, this can be a double-edged sword. When a public company loses such a client, it can immediately become unprofitable and the stock price can drop dramatically. I am always cautious of companies that have a high degree of client concentration.

Is the company involved in any lawsuits? If so, how much can it be liable for?

We live in litigious times. Lawsuits can seriously hurt companies. Therefore, you should always read what the company discloses about lawsuits. What I learned over the years is that companies will only disclose what they are absolutely required to by law. You have to take it into your own hands and research the lawsuit yourself to determine whether its outcome may be significant and if so, to what degree. Companies always try to downplay a lawsuit's importance, especially if they are the defendant.

How does the company grow?

As was already mentioned, public companies must keep growing in order to satisfy Wall Street. Because of this pressure, the management might look for growth at any cost. Figure out where the growth is going to come from. Internal growth is preferable. I personally do not like companies that are serial acquirers of companies. There are a lot of problems that can occur with acquisitions.

Which stock exchange is the company listed on?

This might sound like an unnecessary question but it does matter. If the company is trading on the London Stock Exchange, then you need to make sure that your broker allows you to buy stocks from that exchange. Also, if the company is considered to be a small or micro cap company, it might not even trade on the exchange and may instead trade on the OTC Markets, which is not an exchange but a quotation system where broker-dealers trade with each other. Although you might not notice, trading volumes on the OTC Markets are much smaller. This means that if you need to sell in a hurry, you might not be able to do so without taking a big loss.

Is the company profitable?

You already know whether the company is profitable because you checked it during the quick due diligence stage. Now, you want to perform a detailed financial analysis. The goal is to figure out what the profitability will be in the future because what happened in the past is over. This requires a deep understanding of the business and its prospects. Also, you need to be able to read financial statements. If you don't know how to read and interpret financial statements, read my book, *The Basics of Understanding Financial Statements.*

Is the company growing revenues and net profits every year?

Every 10-K includes financial statements from several years. Companies are required to show you the income statements from the last five years. This allows you to clearly see whether revenues and profits are growing. However, what is more important than just seeing them grow or not grow is the reason behind it because things don't just happen. Financial statements are a way for companies to show you the score. To see how the game was played, you have to read the management's comments throughout the 10-K filing.

Does the company have any debt?

Again, you already know whether there is any debt or not. In this section, you want to find out what kind of debt it is and how it came to be. You want to know the term of the debt, the interest rate, and the maturity date. Is the term two years or 10 years? Is the interest rate in line with the market or is it very high? If it is high, then maybe refinancing will create value by lowering the interest expense.

You want to know why the company acquired this debt. Was it to finance a business acquisition or expansion? If so, was this a smart move? I can't tell you how many times companies take on debt during good times and then struggle with it when the market turns. Companies in cyclical industries are notorious for that. They borrow at the top of the cycle and then go bankrupt at the bottom. Avoid companies that borrow at the top of the cycle. How do you know? If the company is involved in oil, gold, or any other commodity that goes in cycles and it borrows a lot of money when the market is hot, think about selling or not buying the stock.

With that being said, if you find a company that borrows at the bottom of the cycle, then you might make a lot of money when good times come.

If so, is any of this debt coming due soon?

Debt instruments can be structured in various ways. The monthly payments may include repayment of the principal, or they may not. If they do not, the loan must be repaid sometime in the future. This date is disclosed in the company's 10-K filings. Look at the amount that will be due and estimate whether the company will be able to pay it off with its cash flow. If not, then you had better have a reason to believe that there will be no problem refinancing it; otherwise, the stock price will plunge.

After you read the most recent 10-K filing and answer these questions, pull up the 10-K filings from the last 10 years and read them all. The reason why you want to read 10-K filings from many years is so that you can see the company's progression from one year to another. Pay attention to certain things such as projections from previous years. Check to see if they ever came to fruition. If they didn't, why not? Did they miss projections because of the recession or is the management known for overpromising and under delivering?

Take the company's financial data from the last 10 years of 10-K filings and enter it into a Microsoft Excel spreadsheet so that it is easy to analyze. I usually enter only the income statement and balance sheet. This is enough to show me how the company has evolved financially.

Then, once I have this information entered, I analyze it and value the company. Because these are separate topics, I will not be covering them here. This book is about the due diligence process, not financial analysis or valuation. I have separate books on these topics.

Form 10-Q

You don't have to read all of the company's 10-Q filings, which are quarterly reports, because it will take you forever, but you should read the ones that were filed since the most recent 10-K. Obviously, 10-Q filings are shorter than 10-K filings because they cover a shorter time period.

Pay attention to how the balance sheet has changed since the last reporting period. Is it stronger, with more cash, or weaker, with more debt? Look at how the income statement for the quarter compares with the same quarter from the previous year. Does it look like the company is performing as expected or did the business deteriorate? Read the management's explanation about what happened during the three months covered by the report.

DEF 14A

DEF 14A is a document called a definitive proxy statement. It must be filed with the SEC on behalf of a registrant when a shareholder vote is required. You should read it because it tells you who the managers and directors are, how much money they make, what committees they serve on, and how much of the company's stock they own. Some investors think that the proxy document should be read first because it helps you determine whether the company is run for the benefit of the shareholders or the managers.

I study the compensation table carefully and try to answer the following questions:

How much is the CEO making in relation to the CEOs of competing companies?

I don't mind when a CEO makes good money, but I want to know how his compensation compares to the CEOs of competing companies. If the subject company is doing much better than its competitors, then yes, the higher compensation is justified, but if the subject company is on the brink of bankruptcy while its CEO is the highest paid in the industry, then there is a problem. Clearly, the company is being run for the benefit of someone other than the shareholders.

How much is the CEO making in relation to the company's bottom line?

At the end of the day, what matters for any business is the bottom line. Profit is what drives entrepreneurs. The job of the CEO is to manage the company in a way so that shareholders benefit from their ownership. This usually means generating a profit. There is a problem when the CEO's compensation is bigger than the shareholders' profit. Who is the business supposed to benefit, the CEO or the shareholders?

How much is the CEO making in relation to other members of the management team?

The CEO is the most important member of the management team but he relies on the other members in order to do his job. Yes, the CEO should make more money, but the compensation should not be ridiculously skewed towards him. For example, if the CEO makes $10 million per year while the rest of the management team each get paid $100,000 per year, then the company is a one-man show. I don't want to have anything to do with a company like this.

Is the management's compensation in any way tied to the performance of the business?

It really annoys me when I see management teams that pay themselves more and more every year even when their business is struggling. If I see that the business is struggling, then I expect the management to sacrifice and take pay cuts. This shows honesty and integrity. This is the kind of management team that I want to be associated with.

Conference Calls

Sometimes in the Investor Relations section of the company's website, you will have recordings of old conference calls. You should listen to several of them to get to know the company, the management, and how the management communicates with analysts and shareholders. Do they sound promotional, which could be a red flag, or do they sound intelligent and conservative, which is much more preferable? You have to use your judgment here. At the end of a conference call, there is a question and answer session with investors and analysts. This is a time when you can learn about various concerns that shareholders or analysts have for the company's future.

Unfortunately, many times companies do not have any recordings available for you to listen to. Go to SeekingAlpha.com, which you previously visited, and enter the company's ticker symbol. Look at the transcripts section to see if there are any conference calls in text format and read them.

Book about the Company

Previously, I told you that you should learn about the company's industry by reading books about industry-specific topics. You should also search to see if anyone has written a book about your subject company. The type of companies you chose to invest in will often determine whether any books have been written about them. For example, if you want to invest in well known large cap companies such as Coca-Cola, McDonald's, or ExxonMobil, then you will probably find plenty of books on them. However, if you chose to invest in smaller companies, you probably will not have as much luck, but this doesn't mean you shouldn't try. For example, have you heard of Arctic Cat? Arctic Cat manufactures snowmobiles and ATVs. It is a very small company in relation to Coca-Cola or McDonald's, but when you search Amazon, you will find a book about it titled *Legend, Arctic Cat's First Four Decades*, by C.J. Ramstad. Before I invested in Arctic Cat, which by the way turned out to be a 10-bagger, I found this book instrumental. I learned about the company's history, its fight for survival, and many other things that allowed me to understand it better and feel comfortable in investing in it.

Investigate the Management Team

The people that are running your subject company are instrumental in making it successful. As a shareholder, you expect them to be honest and competent. If you had a choice between the following two managers which one would you prefer to run your company?

Manager 1

Joe Smith has served as our president and chief executive officer since 1999. Mr. Smith has more than 25 years of experience in the energy industry. In addition to his responsibilities as president and CEO, Mr. Smith also sits on the board of directors of Company ABS, Company HXR, and Company IPR. In his free time, he enjoys hockey and taking walks with his beautiful daughter.

Manager 2

Joe Smith is a very dishonest man. He cheated his way through high school because he never really enjoyed doing school work. He got into an Ivy League school because of his father's connections. Unsuccessful in getting a real job, he went to work for his father's firm that was founded in 1975. He recently married his third wife, who is 30 years younger than him. The first two marriages did not work because Mr. Smith could not stay away from strip clubs. In 2012, Mr. Smith was arrested for a DUI and fined $2,000. He lives in a $20 million mansion.

I think the answer is obvious, but these biographical descriptions might be of the same person. The first one would be published in the company's proxy document and the second one would never be published. The second description is what you could write after a little bit of investigative work. While his actions may not necessarily be illegal, they reflect his character and judgment.

It is amazing that most investors don't even bother to read beyond the biographical descriptions that are provided to them by the companies themselves. Actually, they don't even bother to read the biographical descriptions at all. They simply assume that the people running public companies are honest. Did you know that Scott Thompson, the former CEO of Yahoo, faked his computer science college degree on his résumé? No one knew until Daniel Loeb pointed it out, and then he had to step down. How come Wall Street analysts didn't know this?

I want to know as much as I can dig up about the members of the management team, especially the CEO. Here are some of the things I want to know:

- What kind of house does he live in and does he own more than one?
- What kind of car does he drive?
- Does he have any criminal history?
- Was he involved in any lawsuits?
- Did he ever declare personal bankruptcy?
- Did any of his previous companies go bankrupt?

- Has he ever been divorced? If so, how many times?
- Did he really graduate from where he says he graduated from?

In order to answer questions like these, you can either find the original source yourself or use a background search provider with an aggregated database. It is most likely best to use a combination of the two. Before we start answering these questions individually, let me give you some background on how the information we want is stored.

Background Checks and the Fair Credit Reporting Act

If you want to investigate someone's background, your first thought might be to find a website where you can purchase a background report. However, before you go about doing this, you need a certain amount of understanding about the background check and consumer reporting industry.

There are two general categories of companies that provide background reports. One includes consumer reporting agencies (CRAs), which, as defined by the Fair Credit Reporting Act (FCRA), provide information on a consumer's creditworthiness, character, general reputation, personal characteristics, or lifestyle in order to determine a consumer's eligibility for specific purposes that have been deemed permissible under the FCRA. The other category includes those whose services fall outside of services regulated by the FCRA.

Consumer reports can contain information such as a person's credit history, criminal records, or even, in the case of "investigative" consumer reports, information from interviews with the consumer's neighbors, friends, or acquaintances.

CRAs, those who use their information, and those who furnish information to them all must comply with the FCRA. The FCRA generally applies to situations where a consumer applies for something, like employment, insurance, or some other kind of service or benefit, and risks being denied because of information contained in a background check. To protect consumers, the FCRA requires employers, lenders, and other users of consumer reports to obtain permission from the consumer, meaning the potential employee or customer, to conduct the background check. Consumers also have the right to obtain a copy of the report and dispute any information that may be incorrect.

Unfortunately, companies that are considered to be consumer reporting agencies and that are required to comply with the FCRA will not provide reports to you for the purpose of researching a corporate executive, mainly because you will not be able to obtain permission from him to conduct the background check.

However, companies that fall outside of these parameters, such as PeopleSmart or Intelius, will provide background searches for you, but the results will consist only of publicly available information that you could theoretically compile yourself. This type of a search is known as "people search" in the industry and is intended for personal use. The benefit is that you do not have to find all the different sources yourself. They will do it for you. Common uses for "people search" background checks include researching a blind date, a potential roommate, or a neighbor.

To make it all a bit more complicated, some companies provide some services that are subject to the FCRA and other services that are not. The FCRA is a long document that is not easy to read and has some gray areas. The Federal Trade Commission determines whether someone has violated the FCRA on a case by case basis.

Background Check Websites

Which background check website should you use? There are many out there and it is up to you to choose one that is reputable. You should be wary of any site that makes promises that are too good to be true. A reputable site will be upfront about its pricing and what information they provide. A poor site may have old information or a limited database. It is easy for them to just take your money and say that no records were found.

One example of a background check site is PeopleSmart, which offers an unlimited search membership for $19.95 per month. If you sign up for quarterly or annual memberships, the price is lower. Intelius is a site that offers unlimited people search reports for a 24-hour period for a one-time fee. It also offers Intelius Premier for a seven-day trial period for a one-time fee, or a subscription for $19.95 per month. Other sites include Instant Checkmate, which provides individual reports as well as access via monthly subscriptions, and BeenVerified, which offers one-, three- and six-month memberships.

Your alternative to a background check website is to hunt down each record yourself. Let's return to our questions and see how to do this.

What kind of house does he live in and does he own more than one?

This is important to me. I do not like when the CEOs of my companies are flashy millionaires unless, of course, they founded the company and they earned it. I mostly invest in small cap companies and I want my CEOs to be motivated to work. If they are filthy rich, what is the motivation to show up and work hard? Also, if they spend money on million-dollar houses, they are probably not careful with money when they run my business.

Addresses can often be found through publicly available sources. Sites that can be helpful include Whitepages.com; genealogy research websites, such as FamilyTreeNow.com; or county assessors, treasurers, and recorders of deeds. Once you find an address, you can look at pictures, descriptions, and estimated values on Zillow, Redfin, and Trulia. Remember, however, that estimates of value on these sites can be inaccurate. According to Zillow's website, its estimated values have a median error rate of 8%.

Another option is to check county records. On the assessor's site, you can find basic data on the property and often a photo. You will also see the assessed value of the property. However, you should remember that the assessed value is often much less than the market value. The assessed value is used to determine the property tax, while the market value represents what a buyer would pay on the open market.

You can also check for records of recent sales with the assessor or the recorder of deeds. Sale prices are public record in some states but not in others. They can be a good indication of market value, assuming the sales were between unrelated parties and free of any special conditions. If you cannot find useful information on the exact property you are researching, you can look at the neighbors' houses, which will often be similar.

What kind of car does he drive?

I believe that a car can reflect someone's personality and values. Which car would you prefer your CEO to drive?

A) Porsche or Lamborghini
B) Honda or Toyota
C) Hummer

If you want a CEO that needs to show his wealth and success to everybody that comes in contact with him, then go with A or C. But if you want a CEO that is cost conscious, then you will choose B. When I was a little boy, I wanted to drive the best-looking cars. However, when I grew up, I realized that money can be better spent in other ways, rather than on a depreciating asset. The problem with some men is that they never grew up and inside, they are still little boys that need the outside world to give them approval. I want nothing to do with a CEO like that.

It is not easy to identify the type of car a CEO drives through public records. The Driver's Privacy Protection Act (DPPA) was passed in 1994 in response to several serious crimes that were committed using personal information that was, at the time, publicly available through motor vehicle records. As a result, unless the person gives written consent, state DMVs can only release personal information from motor vehicle records for specific purposes, such as to law enforcement agencies conducting police work, or insurance companies investigating claims.

There are a few instances where you can obtain a description of a vehicle that someone drives through public records. For example, vehicle accident reports are considered public record in some places, and they contain the names and addresses of the drivers, descriptions of the vehicles involved, and other information.

You may be able to find out about the CEO's car through other publicly available sources. However, public records research is an entire industry that is beyond the scope of this book. If you want to learn more, there are several books on the topic, such as *The Sourcebook to Public Record Information: The Comprehensive Guide to County, State, and*

Federal Public Record Sources, by Michael Sankey, and blogs, such as PI Buzz.

As always, you can try a simple Internet search to try to find out what kind of car he drives. You can check photos on social media sites or Google images, and you can look at a street view of his house on Google Maps to see if there is a car in the driveway. When I perform scuttlebutt research, which I will cover later, the type of car is one of my questions.

Does he have any criminal history?

Next, we wanted to know whether our CEO has had any run-ins with the law. If you know where he lives, you can check the local court system for records of any crimes he committed. However, the problem with criminal records is that they only reflect what occurred in a particular jurisdiction. If the crime happened outside of the court jurisdiction that you are checking, then you will never find it.

It would be easiest to just search one complete and up-to-date database that lists every single criminal record in the United States. That is how it is portrayed in crime dramas on TV and in movies. The boss tells his employee to run a search and after a few taps on the keyboard, the employee has everything the boss wants to know and more. However, no such database exists, even for law enforcement. The largest database of criminal records is the FBI's National Crime Information Center (NCIC), and it is only available to authorized users such as criminal justice agencies, not the general public. And although it is the nation's largest database, it is not complete.

There are many types of criminal records stored in many different locations. Some examples are arrest records and booking files made by local police, county sheriffs, state troopers, the FBI, and US marshals; inmate records created by jails and prisons; and special registries, such as sex offender, abuse, or violent offender registries. Local law enforcement agencies and local courts feed records to state repositories, and states and other entities feed records to the FBI's database. Not all statewide repositories receive complete information from every single county. Furthermore, the information in any database is only as accurate as the person adding it at the time the record is created. Some records lack sufficient detail, and databases are always stale to some degree because there is a delay before they are updated from the original source.

One of the NCIC's sources, the Interstate Identification Index system (III), has final disposition information for only about 50% of its arrest records, according to a special report issued in 2006 by the United States Attorney General. A disposition is the final action in a case, such as a conviction, acquittal, or dismissal of charges. At the state level, approximately 70 to 80 percent of records include final dispositions.

Since the largest criminal records database in the US is incomplete, imagine how complete a database compiled by a private vendor will be? They obtain their records by buying in bulk, sometimes on an annual basis, from middlemen or from law enforcement agencies, courts, and corrections departments, which may be selective about what they provide. Sometimes records that have been expunged in the legal system live on in a private vendors' database for some time. However, such a database may help you find information you wouldn't have found otherwise. Then, you can confirm it with the actual court records.

Once you have identified what locations you want to search, you will know whether you want to search the federal court system or local or state courts. For the federal court system, you can use PACER (Public Access to Court Electronic Records), which is a government-run website that provides to access to US district, bankruptcy and appellate court records and documents. It is mostly used by lawyers, but you can get an account as an individual. When you check local and state court systems, you may also want to check the attorney general's website to see if they have additional records. Recordsproject.com/criminal and

Recordsproject.com/court are links that list how to access criminal records and court records, respectively, for each state.

Was he involved in any lawsuits?

When you hear the term lawsuit, you might only be thinking of a civil lawsuit, but the term just refers to any case that comes before a court, whether civil or criminal. In criminal lawsuits, a person is charged and prosecuted for committing a crime. He may face jail time, a fine, or both. The purpose of a civil lawsuit is to settle a dispute between private parties, and the result is usually monetary damages or orders to do or not do something.

Just like for criminal records research, you can search local and state court records systems, or PACER, for federal records. Also, a simple Google search for the person's name plus "lawsuit" can return pretty good results.

Did he ever declare personal bankruptcy?

Filing for personal bankruptcy is not a crime and it would not make me skip a company if its CEO had done so. This is especially true if the bankruptcy was caused by medical bills or something of that nature. However, if the personal bankruptcy was caused by credit card overspending on luxury items, then this is a different story. The person clearly does not know how to manage his personal finances, so why should he be able to manage those of a publicly traded company?

All bankruptcy cases are handled through the federal court system, and there are federal bankruptcy courts all over the country. Use PACER for this search, too.

Did any of his previous companies go bankrupt?

Since we are on the topic of bankruptcies, it is useful to find out if the manager was involved in companies that previously filed for bankruptcy. Again, you will use PACER for this search. Also, don't forget that a simple Google search can work miracles, too.

Has he ever been divorced? If so, how many times?

Unfortunately, many marriages end up in divorces. If your CEO has been through several divorces, then he might have a problem with commitment, conflict resolution, or all sorts of other issues.

Divorce records are created by local authorities. They are not considered to be federal records. To find divorce records, you can check state and county courts or use online divorce records providers. Some states provide divorce records through the state's department of health, or its equivalent, while others refer you to county clerks, recorders, or courts. Some states make it easy to download long lists of all divorces for a particular year while others require you to submit a request one at a time. You can also use sites like FamilyTreeNow.com or even just search on Google. In Google, search "Person's Name divorce records," or "Person's Name wife/husband."

The Centers for Disease Control and Prevention website lists where to write for vital records, which includes divorce records, at Cdc.gov/nchs/w2w.htm. Recordsproject.com/divorce/ lists how to access divorce records for each state.

Did he really graduate from where he says he graduated from?

To verify someone's education, you can simply call the registrar's office of the school in question and provide them with the person's name. However, if you aren't familiar with the school, you may want to check to make sure it isn't a "diploma mill," which is a company that sells phony degrees on the Internet. You can search the US Department of Education's Ope.ed.gov/Accreditation to verify whether an institution has been accredited by a legitimate accrediting agency.

Social Media Search

Social networking sites can provide information that cannot be found anywhere else. Users may make posts that reveal racist views or illegal drug use, or they may complain about their jobs. There are not very many background search companies that provide information from social networking sites. A few established companies have added social media searches to the services they already provide. However, it is a growing part of the business and some new companies that specialize in background reports derived from social media are forming. The information that companies take from social networking sites to provide to their clients must be publicly available. They cannot use information that was posted privately.

One of the first to establish itself was Social Intelligence (SocialIntel.com). While Social Intelligence is considered a consumer reporting agency that complies with the FCRA, it also provides two people search products that you as an investor can use. One is the Due Diligence Report product, which is a $150 report created by the company. It can be purchased one report at a time. The other option is Underwriting Workbench, which is a service provided through a monthly subscription. The basic version is $199 per month for unlimited searches and reports.

These are some examples of how I investigate members of the management team. You can obviously do a lot more in-depth research than what I just described, but most of the time, you will find out enough just by following these simple steps. If you want to become good at investigating, think like an investigator. Read articles and books on the subject. Call some of them and ask for resources that they use. For example, some investigators use services like Arachnys.com, LexisNexis's Accurint, or Thomson Reuters' CLEAR online. These are powerful products, but they also cost a lot of money. Also, Scip.org (Strategic and Competitive Intelligence Professionals) can help you find resources on how to become a better investigator.

Get Reviews—Scuttlebutt

Before you buy a high-end camera, you are likely going to read reviews about the product before you spend a significant chunk of money on it. You should do the same before buying a stock. Get reviews or references from people that are involved with the company such as current or former employees, other investors, and customers. This is referred to as scuttlebutt research. It was popularized by Philip Fisher and described in his book, *Common Stocks and Uncommon Profits*. I also wrote a book called *Scuttlebutt Investor* where I go into great detail about how I do scuttlebutt research.

The term scuttlebutt originally referred to a barrel used to store drinking water on sailing ships. "Butt" referred to the barrel and "scuttle" meant to chop or drill a hole as for tapping a cask. Sailors would gather around the scuttlebutt to drink water and as they did, they exchanged gossip, just the way people do today around water coolers in offices. Eventually, the term scuttlebutt came to refer to not just the barrel, but also to the rumors and gossip.

The idea behind the scuttlebutt method is to get people who know about the company to share their knowledge with you so that you gain a better understanding of the underlying business and the people that are running it. The four main groups of people that you are trying to gather feedback from are current or former employees, customers, suppliers, and managers.

Current employees are easy to locate. You can either walk into the place of business or you can find them on LinkedIn. If they work in the company's retail store, just start talking to them. If they work in the company's office, call them on the phone. Also, you can get feedback through Glassdoor.com, which we previously discussed. Another way is to use a graph search on Facebook, such as "geologists who work at Barrick Gold Corporation."

Here are some of the questions that you want to ask:

- What is it like or what was it like to work for the company?
- Does the management treat its employees with respect?
- Do you like or dislike like working there and why?
- How does the company promote people?
- Does it promote from within (this is preferable) or does it hire people from outside?
- Are employees properly compensated?
- How is the employee turnover?
- Would you recommend this company to any of your friends?

It has been my experience that, as you might expect, current employees will tell you some information, but former employees will tell you more. You can ask them the same questions. There are more ways to find former employees than I can list here, but I will give you some examples. You can use Archive.org to look up past versions of the company's website and find the names of any employees that were listed. On LinkedIn, under advanced search, search for "past not current" employees, or look through resume database websites. You can also use the unofficial Facebook advanced search engine SearchIsBack.com and narrow your search by current or former company. Both current and former employees may follow the company via social media sites, commenting on posts or showing up in pictures.

You can also seek out membership lists from professional organizations or bulletins from past conferences. Old newspaper or magazine articles about the company may mention the names of employees. Corporate filings with the Secretary of State, SEC filings, and old annual reports usually include lists of current and past officers, directors, and managers. Each state issues professional licenses for various professions and you can look them up online through whichever department oversees it for that state. If the company was ever involved in any litigation, you may find the names of former employees listed in the court documents.

Customers are a bit trickier to locate. However, sometimes the companies list them in the 10-K filings or investor presentations. If not, you can still locate them by asking around or by using Google to search. Here are some of the questions that I want to ask the customers:

- Are they satisfied with the product or service?

- Why are they buying from the subject company?
- How long have they been a customer?
- What kind of problems do the company's products or services solve for them?

To locate the suppliers, you need to put yourself in the shoes of the subject company? What kind of supplies do I need in order to produce what I am selling? Then, search for the companies that supply those kinds of items. From suppliers, you want to find out answers to the following questions.

- What kind of experience do they have working with the subject company?
- How long have they been supplying to the subject company?
- Are they the only supplier? If so, can the subject company find a replacement supplier if needed?
- Is the supplier able to profit from doing business with the subject company?
- Can the supplier easily pass on cost increases to the subject company?
- How does the subject company compare to its competitors that the supplier works with?

In addition to getting feedback from these four main groups, you should also get some feedback from other investors. You can visit various message boards where smaller investors hang out. To contact the serious investors, like hedge funds, you need to use a different route because usually they do not post on message boards even though they might read them. To find them, search for filings of Schedules 13D and 13G on EDGAR under the subject company's ticker symbol. Also, you can find the names of the largest shareholders in the proxy document. Call them up and ask them the following questions:

- What has been your experience with owning the company?
- Is the management open to talking with you?
- Why did you invest in the company?
- What do you like and dislike about the company?
- What do you think the stock should trade for within the next three years?
- Is this a big position in relation to your entire portfolio?

Locating the management team is the easiest. They are listed in the proxy documents. By now, you should know a lot about the company and whether the stock is cheap enough for you to buy it. But before you do so, call the company and ask if you can talk to the CEO, CFO, and/or COO. If it is a big company, then you most likely will have no shot at getting to talk to them. If that is the case, ask to talk to an Investor Relations representative. But if you are dealing with a small company, you will most likely get the CEO on the phone. Tell the person that you are interested in buying stock in the company and that you have studied it for the last several days but that you would like to ask a few more questions. Most CEOs love talking about themselves and their businesses so once you get them going you might be on the phone for an hour.

Before giving you some questions to ask, I would like to point out why you want to interview the CEO at the end of your due diligence process. One reason is that by now you know a lot about the company and you can actually have an intelligent conversation. You probably know what to ask when the CEO responds to something, and you might be able to come up with another question on the spot. Another reason why you want to talk to the CEO at the end is the fact that many of them are excellent salespeople and if you spoke with them at the beginning, they might sell you on the company. You could end up buying the stock without completing the full due diligence process.

When I get CEOs on the phone, I usually like to start the conversation with something like:

- How did you get into this business?
- Was it something that you always wanted to do or did you just happen to get into it by accident?
- How are you different from your competitors?
- Why do customers buy from you instead of your competitors?
- Do you have any competitive advantages?
- What kind of challenges, if any, did you experience over the last five years?
- What kind of challenges, if any, is the company experiencing right now?
- Where do you see your company in five to 10 years?
- What are your plans for growing the company?
- Are you looking at any acquisitions?
- When you make acquisitions, what do you look for in the target companies?
- What prices are you willing to pay for them?
- What is your philosophy on capital allocation?

These are some basic questions that you might ask but conversations never go according to plan. The best thing is to just let the conversation happen and slip your questions in when you can. You will already have the answers to many of these questions, but you want to hear it again from the CEO to see if his answers are consistent with what you already learned before. Also, you might have other questions that I did not list here. Don't be shy, just ask.

Many investors are shy about talking to employees, customers, or managers of the company, and this is understandable, but these conversations are extremely helpful in understanding the company and the people that are affected by it. Not all of them will talk to you. You will be rejected, but this doesn't matter. If you try to talk to enough people, in the end you will come out ahead because you will have gained a great deal from the ones who were willing to talk.

CHAPTER 5

Conclusion

CHAPTER 5

Conclusion

In this book, I gave you a road map of what you need to do in terms of research before you buy the stock of a particular company. First, you complete the quick due diligence stage where you check some basic facts to see if you are somewhat interested in pursuing the company. Then, you spend a little bit more time on the medium due diligence stage to familiarize yourself more with the investment opportunity. And finally, when the first two steps have a positive outcome, then you engage in full due diligence which is much more intense and time consuming. In this step, you learn about the industry by reading books and articles, or by watching YouTube videos. You learn about the company by reading various SEC documents such as filings of Forms 10-K and 10-Q, and by talking to employees, investors, customers, suppliers, and managers.

If, after your due diligence, you still like the company and the stock is trading at a cheap or reasonably cheap price, you buy it for your portfolio. If you like the company but you think that the price is too high, you put it on your watch list and keep waiting until the price becomes low enough for you to buy it. If you don't like the company or its price, then you simply move on.

Other Books by this Author

Other Books by this Author

The following is a list of other books written by Mariusz Skonieczny:

- *Why Are We So Clueless about the Stock Market?*
- *The Basics of Understanding Financial Statements*
- *100 Ways to Find Investment Ideas*
- *Gold Production from Beginning to End*
- *Investment Wisdom*
- *Scuttlebutt Investor*

Made in the USA
Lexington, KY
03 November 2019